The Thanksgiving Book

FULL OF THE SEASON'S
HISTORY - POEMS - SONGS
ART PROJECTS - GAMES - RECIPES

**For Parents and Teachers to use
with young Children.**

**Written and Illustrated by
SUSAN OLSON HIGGINS**

Ask for these additional holiday books
by the same Author:
THE PUMPKIN BOOK
THE BUNNY BOOK
THE ELVES' CHRISTMAS BOOK

PUMPKIN PRESS

P.O. Box 139
Shasta, CA 96087

5th Edition, Copyright © 1984 by Susan Olson Higgins

Written and Published by Susan Olson Higgins
P.O. Box 139, Shasta, CA 96087

ISBN 0939973-01-4

Dedicated to those snowy, cold trips to Norwood Park for wonderful family gatherings and Thanksgiving feasts; and to someone I dearly love and am most thankful for . . . my mother.

I'd like to take this opportunity to give thanks to those who contributed so much of their time, talent and expertise to **The Thanksgiving Book.**

Thank you: Dan Higgins, Dorothy Jane Williams, Joyce Huber, Dick Burns, Mary Burns, and especially V.I. Wexner for editing this collection.

PREFACE

Thanksgiving is such a special time to remember all the blessings we have.

Within these pages are history, poems, songs, art projects, games and recipes for you to use when you gather together with loved ones and friends for this holiday.

Have a Happy Thanksgiving!

Susan Olson Higgins

Gobble...Gobble all you can this Thanksgiving!

TABLE OF CONTENTS

1

THE HISTORY OF THANKSGIVING

September 6, 1620, a small group of brave men, women, and children left Plymouth, England, seeking a new homeland where they could worship God as they pleased. They boarded two small vessals, the Speedwell and the Mayflower, and set sail for a new land, America.

It wasn't long before the Speedwell developed a leak and was forced to return to England. But the Mayflower continued its courageous voyage across the ocean. Finally, two months later, the Mayflower landed at Provincetown, Massachusetts on November 11, 1620. The colonists left the ships and continued on to found their settlement in Plymouth, Massachusetts.

The first winter was very harsh. It was terribly cold and there were not enough supplies or food. The colonist had not had time to build adequate shelters before winter conditions set in. Many colonists died that first winter.

In the spring, the Wampanoag Indians befriended the Pilgrims and came to their settlement to help them plant wheat, as well as corn, beans, pumpkins, and other vegetables. They also taught them ways to survive and hunt in this new land.

In the fall of 1621, the crops were ready for harvest and it looked as if there would be enough food to last the winter. The Pilgrims decided to celebrate by giving a harvest party. They invited the Wampanoag Indians to join them.

There were not enough tables and chairs, so some had to sit on the ground. Their plates were made of wood and not all of the people had silverware. The children played together, racing, wrestling, and dressing homemade cornhusk dolls.

The food was plentiful. The Indians brought five deer as gifts to their hosts. The Pilgrims served corn, beans, stewed pumpkins, corn cakes, berries and nuts gathered from the woods, succotash, and frumenty (a dish of wheat boiled in milk). They also served roast goose, deer, turkey, duck and fish. The children helped by turning the meat on the spit over the fire.

Although the Pilgrims certainly did have much to be thankful for, at that time they believed that religious ceremonies should be held at a separate time and place, away from feasts, celebrations, or parties. The religious theme was added to Thanksgiving later on.

After that first celebration, Thanksgiving was held on many different dates and days. In 1863, Abraham Lincoln proclaimed that last Thursday in November as "a day of thanksgiving and praise to our beneficient Father." Then, in 1939, President Roosevelt set the date one week earlier to lengthen the shopping period before Christmas. Finally, in 1941, the fourth Thursday of November was set by Congress as the federal holiday of Thanksgiving.

TURKEY FACTS

Our domestic turkey is the direct descendant of the wild turkey found in the Americas when the Pilgrims arrived in 1620. In fact, the turkey is the only poultry which is native to this country. Early settlers and Indians enjoyed delicious wild turkey meat, then used the feathers for blankets or headgear.

Of the six varieties of turkeys, the most popular is called the Standardbred Bronze. Market age is approximately 6 months, at which time the Toms usually weigh an average of 20 pounds. The largest turkey on record weighed 75 pounds! That turkey would have provided a *huge* Thanksgiving feast! M-m-m-m.

INDIAN MAKE-UP

Indians painted their bodies and faces for protection against the sun, wind and insects. Some markings indicated political and religious societies, or deeds an Indian accomplished. Often the decorations had no meaning, but were merely designs. However color usually had a significant meaning. For example, painting faces white usually symbolized the wolf whose powers were considered to be great when out scouting.

Colors for the make-up were made from berries, bark, and the fruit of plants or shrubs. These were dried and made into powders. The Indians stored the colored powder in pouches which they carried with then at all times. If one needed protection from the elements, he would rub grease from the fat of a buffalo-back into his palm, then onto his face. Then he would put his greasy fingers into his pouch of colored powder and rub the powder onto his face. The color would adhere to the buffalo fat and cover his face evenly.

INDIAN SIGNS

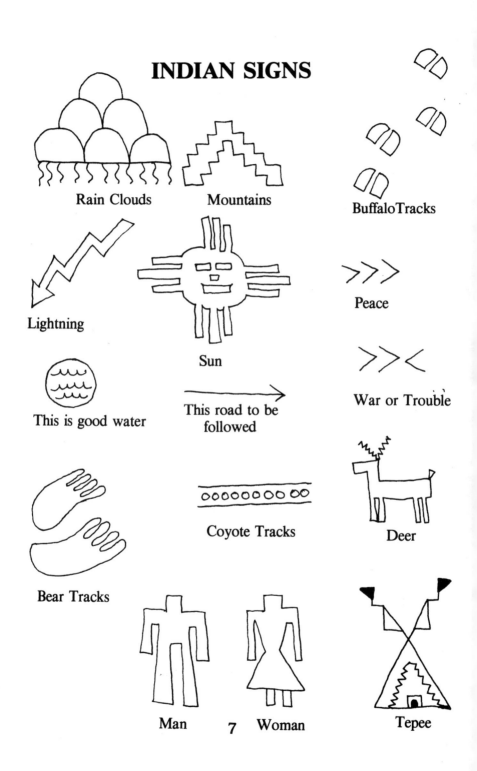

Rain Clouds

Mountains

BuffaloTracks

Lightning

Sun

Peace

This is good water

This road to be
followed

War or Trouble

Bear Tracks

Coyote Tracks

Deer

Man

7

Woman

Tepee

POEMS TO GOBBLE UP

GETTING READY FOR THE FIRST THANKSGIVING

by Susan Olson Higgins

Churn that butter. *(pretend to churn)*
Pick that corn. *(put corn in basket)*
Polish father's *(pretend to rub)*
Old brass horn.

Pluch those feathers. *(pluch duck's feathers)*
Clean those fish. *(pretend to scale them)*
Chisel another *(pretend to chisel)*
Wooden dish.

Bring more wood. *(pretend to carry)*
Stir those coals. *(pretend to stir)*
Spoon the succotash *(pretend to spoon)*
Into bowls.

Cook the pumpkin. *(pretend to stir)*
Turn the meat. *(pretend to turn spit)*
It is nearly *(rub your tummy)*
Time to eat.

Our Indian guests *(points)*
Will soon be here. *(point to floor)*
Someone slice *(pretend to carve)*
The leg of deer.

FIRST THANKSGIVING OF ALL

By Nancy Byrd Turner

Peace and Mercy and Jonathan
And Patience (very small),
Stood by the table giving thanks,
The first Thanksgiving of all.

There was very little for them to eat,
Nothing special and nothing sweet;
Only bread and a little broth,
And a bit of fruit (and no tablecloth);

But, Peace and Mercy and Jonathan
And Patience, in a row
Stood up and asked a blessing on
Thanksgiving, long ago.

Thankful they were their ship had come
Safely across the sea;
Thankful they were for hearth and home,
And kin and company;

They were glad of broth to go with their bread,
Glad their apples were round and red,
Glad of mayflowers they would bring
Out of the woods again next spring.

So Peace and Mercy and Jonathan
And Patience (very small);
Stood up gratefully giving thanks,
The first Thanksgiving of all.

THANKSGIVING DAY GATHERING

By Susan Olson Higgins

The doorbell rings.
"We are here," they sing.
We open the door,
And in they pour.
>It has been a whole year.
>We hug and cheer,
>"The cousins and Grandpa
>Are finally here!"

We sit and eat
The turkey meat.
And laugh and chat,
'bout this and that.
>We clear the dishes,
>Make wishbone wishes,
>Eat pumpkin pie,
>And MORE turkey on rye.

Then cousins gather,
To sing and play.
Oh, how I love
Thanksgiving Day!

FIRST THANKSGIVING

by Susan Olson Higgins

Families of Pilgrims came together,
Indians joined them, too.
They ate the first Thanksgiving meal
Beginning tradition for me and you.

11

WHAT IS IT?

by Susan Olson Higgins

Hold only your half
Pinch just so.
Begin to pull
When I say GO.
When it snaps,
Just one of us claps.

What is it?

TOO FULL

by Susan Olson Higgins

My favorite part of Thanksgiving Day,
Is when Dad says, "Put your toys away."
We come to the table and say a blessing,
Pass the turkey and corn and dressing.

We have cranberries, olives, pickles and bread.
Even my kitten is turkey-fed.
My favorite food is pumpkin pie,
With whipped cream mountains piled so high.

When I am done, I leave the table.
But I do not play...I am not able!
(hold tummy)

THANKSGIVING DAY
by Lydia Maria Child

Over the river and through the wood,
    To grandfather's house we go;
The horse knows the way
    To carry the sleigh
Through the white and drifted snow.

Over the river and through the wood,
    Oh, how the wind does blow!
It stings the toes,
    And bites the nose,
As over the ground we go.

Over the river and through the wood,
    To have a first-rate play.
Hear the bells ring,
    "Ting-a-ling-ding!"
Hurrah for Thanksgiving Day!

Over the river and through the wood,
    Trot fast, my dapple-gray!
Spring over the ground,
    Like a hunting-hound!
For this is Thanksgiving Day.

Over the river and through the wood,
    And straight through the barnyard gate;
We seem to go
    Extremely slow,
It is so hard to wait!

Over the river and through the wood,
    Now grandmother's cap I spy!
Hurrah for the fun!
    Is the pudding done?
Hurrah for the pumpkin pie!

TURKEYS MOVE IN THE STRANGEST WAY...

by Susan Olson Higgins

Turkeys move in the strangest way,
    Whenever they go to the forest to play.

Flying to the branches they flutter, flutter,
    flutter,
Walking to the meadow they strut, strut,
    strutter!

Stepping over acorns, they wobble, wobble,
    wobble!
And they NEVER stop talking with a gobble,
    gobble, gobble!

When turkeys hurry to a hiding spot,
They scurry, scurry, scurry with a trot, trot,
    trot!

GOBBLE! GOBBLE!

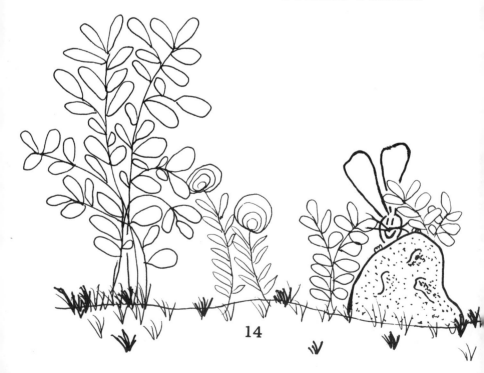

14

THANKSGIVING IN THE FOREST

by Susan Olson Higgins

One sleepy Turkey sitting on a stump,
Saw a fat green Frog on a lily pad jump.

Then out hopped Rabbit, soft, brown and furry,
He didn't stop to talk, for he was in a hurry.

Old red Fox with his bushy red tail,
Came scooting from his den and down the
    forest trail.

Quietly, very quietly, Deer walked by,
Turkey sat and wondered where he went...
    and why?

High overhead, Blue Jay flew away,
He chattered back to Turkey...
    "This is Thanksgiving Day".

So they all came together, every forest beast,
For a friendly and delicious Thanksgiving feast.

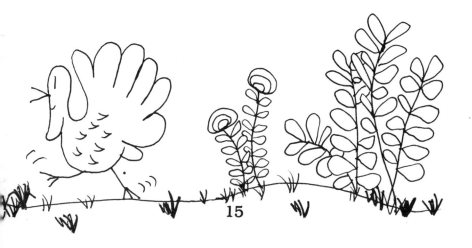

15

FIVE PLUMP TURKEYS

by Susan Olson Higgins

Five plump turkeys full of merriment and fun,
(hold up & spread 5 fingers to represent 5 turkeys)

Sat together on a branch in the sun.
(use forearm held horizontally under turkeys for branch)

The first one said, "It's that time of year."
(wiggle first finger)

The second one said, "A pilgrim's coming near!"
(wiggle second finger)

The third one said, "Oh, it couldn't be so."
(wiggle third finger)

The fourth one said, "I think it's time to go."
(wiggle fourth finger)

The fifth one said, "Come quick, follow me!"
We will run and hide behind the old oak tree."
(wiggle fifth finger)

Away ran the turkeys as fast as they could go.
(wiggle all five fingers as they 'run' behind your back)

Where are they hiding?
(look around)

The Pilgrim doesn't know!
(While the five turkeys stay hidden behind your back, walk two fingers from the other hand through the air to represent the Pilgrim searching for turkeys)

The TOM TOM

by Susan Olson Higgins

Hear the
    tom-tom, tom-tom, tom-tom;
Make a
    pom-pom, pom-pom, pom-pom;
Feet go
    bom-bom, bom-bom, bom-bom;
To the
    tom-tom, tom-tom, tom-tom.

NOTE:
Set the beat before reading this poem by tapping your knee
with your hand.

ONE FAT TURKEY

by Susan Olson Higgins

One fat turkey went strutting by,
He shook his feathers and winked his eye.
He flapped his wings and his head gave a
      wobble,
As he looked at me and said, "Gobble,
      gobble, gobble!"

TURKEYS ON PARADE

by Dick Burns

Here comes the brown turkey
    ruffle, ruffle, ruffle.
Here comes the red turkey
    fluff, fluff, fluffle.
Here comes the orange turkey
    gobble, gobble, gobble.
Here come all the turkeys
    strut, strut, wobble.

*(Make colored feathers for the children
to carry in as each color is read.)*

THREE FAT TURKEYS
ACTION POEM

by Susan Olson Higgins

Choose five children to act out this poem before you begin reading. You will need three turkeys, one child standing by a tree, and one "tree."

Three fat turkeys perched in a tree,
> *(have three 'turkeys' standing in a row)*

One flew down to sit beside me.
> *(have one 'turkey' fly to a child standing near the 'tree')*

Two fat turkeys perched in a tree

One flew down to sit beside me.
> *(have the second 'turkey' fly to the child near the 'tree')*

One fat turkey perched in a tree

He flew down to sit beside me.
> *(have the third 'turkey' fly to the child near the 'tree')*

No fat turkeys perched in a tree

They are all strutting home

In a line behind me!
> *(child and turkeys strut away in a line around the room)*

19

TURKEY RIDDLES
by Dick Burns

What part of the turkey do you find in the orchestra?

(drumstick)

What did the turkey say to the oven?

(Open the door, I'm roasting)

What did the turkey say to the refrigerator?

(Close the door, I'm dressing)

LITTLE BLUEBIRD'S THANKSGIVING
by Susan Olson Higgins

Little Bluebird,
Hop, hop, hop
Peck, peck, peck away.
Eating all the crumbs which dropped
That first Thanksgiving Day.

THE FIRST THANKSGIVING DAY
by Susan Olson Higgins

The pilgrims made a table long
Then gathered 'round for feast and song.

They gathered all to eat and pray
On that very first Thanksgiving Day.

20

WE GATHER TOGETHER
FOR
THANKSGIVING SONGS

This Is The Way On Thanksgiving Day

lyrics by: Susan Olson Higgins
(tune: Mulberry Bush)

This is the way to Grandma's house,
Grandma's house,
Grandma's house,
This is the way to Grandma's house
On Thanksgiving Day.

(point the way)

Additional Verses...

This is the way to drive the car,
(pretend to drive)
This is the way to carve the turkey,
(pretend to carve)
This is the way to say a blessing,
(pretend to pray)
This is the way to eat the pie,
(pretend to eat)
This is the way to clear the table,
(pretend to clear table)
This is the way to sit and play,
(pretend to play)
This is the way to say good-bye,
(wave good-bye)
This is the way to drive back home,
(pretend to drive home)

...on Thanksgiving Day.

Turkey Hide and Seek

lyrics by: Susan Olson Higgins

(tune: Ten Little Indians)

Sing this song once or twice. Choose one boy or girl to be an Indian and one to be a turkey to act out the words as you sing.

Strut through the forest little Turkey
Fly to the tree tops little turkey *(turkey finds hiding spot)*
Hide behind branches little turkey, *(turkey quietly hides)*
An Indian boy is near. *(Indian boy comes in to look for turkey)*

Stalk through the forest little Indian *(Indian boy looks for turkey)*
Hunt for a turkey, little Indian
Search every tree top little Indian
A turkey might be near.

Did little Indian find a turkey? *(if yes, Indian nods head)*
Did little Indian find a turkey?
Did little Indian find a turkey?
Did he find him OVER THERE? *(all children point to the turkey)*

(If little Indian did not find the turkey, everyone in the circle should point to the turkey now.)

23

I'm A Little Turkey

lyrics by: Susan Olson Higgins

(tune: Teapot)

I'm a little turkey, look at me.
Fat and plump as I can be.
Don't you try to catch me
'Cause, you see,
I'll hide behind this old oak tree.

The First Thanksgiving

lyrics by: Susan Olson Higgins

(tune: Twinkle, Twinkle)

Pick the corn and pick the beans,
Pick the squash and other greens.
It is harvest time you see,
Come and share a feast with me.
Bring your family out to play,
We'll call this Thanksgiving Day.

All Around The Table

lyrics by: Susan Olson Higgins

(tune: London Bridges Falling Down)

Peter, Sarah, follow me, follow me,
　　follow me,
Josh and Andrew follow me,
　　'round the table.

(You can substitute other children's names here.)

We will have a turkey feast, turkey feast,
　　turkey feast.
We will have a turkey feast, 'round the table.

Please do pass the pumpkin pie, pumpkin
　　pie, pumpkin pie,
Please do pass the pumpkin pie, 'round the
　　table.

Do you know what day this is, day this is,
　　day this is?
Do you know what day this is?
　　It's Thanksgiving.

26

INDIAN DANCE

1. Set a beat by clapping your hand or tapping a table top with a stick. Every fourth beat should be emphasized or louder. (For example: ONE, two, three, four. ONE, two, three, four.)

2. Demonstrate stepping toe to heel, toe to heel to the beat:

RIGHT FT	LEFT FT	RIGHT FT	LEFT FT
toe, heel	*toe, heel*	*toe, heel*	*toe, heel*
ONE, two	three, four	ONE, two	three, four

3. Draw a pattern on the floor for the dancers to follow.
4. Tap table while dancers dance to your beat.

Variation: Take a step, then stomp toe around side of foot in a forward motion. (For example:
> *Right: step, stomp, stomp, stomp...*
> *Left: step, stomp, stomp, stomp...*
> *Right: step, stomp, stomp, stomp...*

**CORNUCOPIA
OF
ART**

TALL TEEPEE

MATERIALS YOU WILL NEED
    one roll of butcher paper
    6 broomsticks or similar long poles
    tape, glue, string, and staples
    tempera paint and paint brushes
    scissors

WHAT TO DO

1.   Tie the poles together near the top, snuggly and securely. (see illustration)
2.   If possible, masking tape each leg of the teepee to the floor to prevent slipping while you wrap the poles in paper.
3.   Begin wrapping the poles in paper, starting at the top. Tape, glue or staple the paper to the poles as you go. Then wrap paper around the lower half of the poles. Either leave space for a door by folding back the paper, or cut a door once the paper is in place. Trim excess paper away.

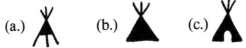

(a.)   (b.)   (c.)

wrap top ½   Wrap bottom ½   trim excess paper

4.   Mix the tempera paint.
5.   Discuss how the Indians used designs and figures to communicate feelings or beliefs or stories about their lives. (See Indian signs, p. 7)
6.   Have each child take a turn painting a design or 'story' on the teepee.

7.   The teepee is a wonderful place for children to go to read a book or to "campout".

29

CLAY AND TOOTHPICK TURKEY

MATERIALS YOU WILL NEED
  modeling clay
  toothpicks

WHAT TO DO
1. To form the turkey's body, roll a small round ball between the palms of your hands with the clay. Save a pinch of clay for the head, beak, and comb. Mold them and attach them to the body.
2. Push about six toothpicks into the clay in a fan-shape for the turkey's tail feathers.
3. Add clay wings.

HORNBOOK

MATERIALS YOU WILL NEED
  one 9x12 sheet of brown construction paper one sheet of lined paper glue scissors

  glue
  scissors
  tagboard

WHAT TO DO
1. Cut a tagboard pattern for a hornbook. Trace around the pattern on brown construction paper and cut out.
2. Cut lined paper 1/2" smaller than hornbook.
3. Give an assignment to be written on the lined paper. Example: write the alphabet; two facts from the social studies text; multiplication facts; or your name.
4. Glue the lined paper on the hornbook.

INDIAN BEADS

MATERIALS YOU WILL NEED
>one strong, large, sharp needle
>heavy duty thread, approximately 24″ long
>a small piece of cardboard
>acorn caps
>any additional material you wish to add to
>>your necklace such as wooden beads,
>>cherrios, buttons, etc.
>an adult to supervise sewing

WHAT TO DO

1. Demonstrate safe use of the needle and lay down safety rules before you begin.
2. Have the children push the needle through the top of the acorn cap into the cardboard while it sits securely on a table top. The children should NOT hold the acorn in hand as they force the needle through the acorn.
3. String as many acorns and other material as desired to make a necklace.
4. Tie the ends of the string together loosely so the child can pull the necklace over his head easily.

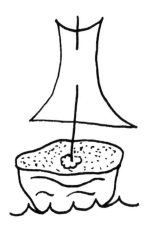

MAYFLOWER SHIP IN A WALNUT SHELL

MATERIALS YOU WILL NEED

> one half of a walnut shell, empty
> one toothpick
> one tiny piece of clay
> one white paper sail

WHAT TO DO

1. Place the clay in the center bottom of the walnut shell.
2. Push the toothpick through the sail in at least two places to hold the sail in place.
3. Push one end of the toothpick into the clay to stand up the sail in the boat.
4. Try sailing your Mayflower boats in a small pan of water.

CROSS-STITCH SAMPLER

MATERIALS YOU WILL NEED
> one 6x12 piece of old sheet or material
> one crayon or magic marker
> masking tape

WHAT TO DO
1. Tape the piece of material down on the desk top.
2. With crayon or magic marker, write your name by placing one 'X' above another, as sewn on a cross-stitch sampler.
3. When you are finished, you may wish to glue the material onto a piece of construction paper for a frame.

PAINT WITH A CORNSTALK

MATERIALS YOU WILL NEED
> one 12" section of corn stalk
> one color of tempera paint
> newsprint or construction paper
> scissors

WHAT TO DO
1. Mix the tempera paint.
2. Trim away excess parts of the corn stalk.
3. Paint the Mayflower, your name, or an Indian design with the corn stalk.

SAWDUST DOLL

MATERIALS YOU WILL NEED

sawdust (about one coffee can full)
two 10"x12" pieces of old sheet
needle and thread and pins
scissors
marking pen
yarn (optional)

OPENING

WHAT TO DO

1. Lay both pieces of material together on the floor.
2. Draw a large, simple outline of a doll. Children might need some direction here.
3. Pin the two pieces of material together.
4. Stitch a short running stitch along the outline you drew for the doll. Be careful to follow safety rules as you sew. Children should not sit close together, and they should stitch with the needle pushing into the floor or a magazine so they will not prick themselves.
5. Stitch all the way around the outline of the doll, except for a 4-5" opening on one leg where the doll can be turned inside out and filled with sawdust.
6. Turn the doll inside out.
7. Fill the doll with sawdust.
8. Stitch the doll to close the opening.
9. If need be, stitch around the doll again to make sure the sawdust does not fall out.
10. Draw eyes, nose and mouth on the doll.
11. If you would like, stitch yarn hair on the doll's head.

PAPER PLATE INDIAN SHIELD

MATERIALS YOU WILL NEED

one paper plate
two feathers (either real or home made) black magic
marker
crayons
scissors
one 2x6" strip of material

WHAT TO DO

1. Divide the plate into four equal sections with the magic marker.
2. Decorate each section by drawing Indian designs with crayons. A sun might be drawn in one section and a lightening bolt in another, for example.

   Insert (or tape) the feathers in one of the bottom sections.
4. With the scissors, puncture a hole in the center of the shield. Pull the material strip through the hole. Tie a knot on either end of the strip to secure the handle of the shield for the child to hold.

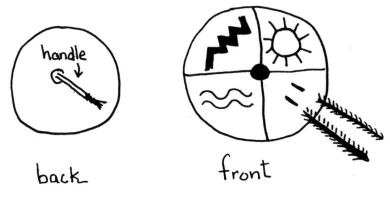

back   front

FEATHER AND INK ART

MATERIALS YOU WILL NEED
real quill feathers
black or blue ink
grocery bags or paper
scissors

WHAT TO DO
1. If you use grocery bags, cut them into 12x12"
   squares.
2. Dip the quill tip into the ink. Gently tap it until all
   of the excess ink is off to avoid drips.
3. On the grocery bag or paper, draw or write
   anything you wish!
4. Remember...the ink will not remain long on the
   tip of the feather, and it will often blotch. You
   may wish to explain this to the young artists so
   they do not become frustrated. Instead, turn it into
   an artistic experience! You might also wish to
   explain that quills were some of the first pens ever
   used. Imagine how difficult it was to write back
   then!

*Variation: Write an Indian story on **wrinkled** brown paper bag
squares. Tear the edges. Use the Indian signs on page 7 to help you tell
a story without using words; or make up signs of your own to tell your
tale. (wrinkled paper looks like leather)*

EXAMPLE:

*One sunny day a deer came
walking by.
It stopped under a tree to
nibble grass.
Then he bounced away over
the river.*

REFRIGERATOR CARTON
L-O-G C-A-B-I-N

MATERIALS YOU WILL NEED

one refrigerator carton, or large cardboard box
one sharp knife
an adult to supervise the cutting
brown tempera paint and brushes
large material scraps
white glue

WHAT TO DO

1. Turn the carton upside down.
2. An adult should cut out a door and windows, using the sharp knife.
3. Paint horizontal strips across each side of the carton to make 'logs' on your log cabin.
4. On the inside, glue a narrow strip of material on both sides of each window for curtains.
5. Enjoy imagining what it would be like to be a Pilgrim living in a log cabin long ago.

STRING, STICK, AND STRAW BROOMS

MATERIALS YOU WILL NEED

long pieces of straw or dried grasses or weeds string
one 2-3 foot stick
scissors

WHAT TO DO

1. Tie small bunches of straw or weeds together at one end with the string. Cut off excess string.
2. Tie all of the small bunches together around the stick very tightly. Wrap the string around and around the bunches and the handle to secure them. Tie a knot and cut off excess string.
3. Be careful! These brooms are not as sturdy as those we buy today!

TOTEM POLE

MATERIALS YOU WILL NEED
    at least three cans the same size
    white glue
    construction paper cut to the size of cans
    yarn scraps
    buttons
    crayons
    scissors
    construction paper scraps

WHAT TO DO
1. Glue the rim or edge of each can. Set one can on top of the other where it is glued.
2. Cover the cans with the construction paper cut to the size of the cans. Glue the paper onto the cans.
3. Decorate each can with a different face, using the yarn, buttons, crayons, and construction paper scraps to create each unique feature.
4. Have a child tell a story about each character on the totem pole.

POPCORN PAINTING

MATERIALS YOU WILL NEED
> a bowl full of popped popcorn
> clean hands
> 9x12" paper
> water, tub, and towel
> pie tin of paint - any color(s)

WHAT TO DO
1. Let the children eat lots of popped popcorn before you even begin!
2. Take one or two kernels of popped popcorn and dip them into the paint.
3. Rub the popcorn across the paper to make any design. The popcorn will get very soggy. Some of it will stick to the paper. That is all right. It will add texture to the picture.
4. When popcorn painting is finished, dip messy hands in the water tub to clean them, then dry them on the towel.
5. You might mention that it was the Indians who taught the Pilgrims how to make popcorn.

BOW AND ARROW

MATERIALS YOU WILL NEED
   one green stick approximately 3 feet long
   one straight stick approximately 2 feet long
   one string approximately 3 feet long
   scissors
   two paper arrow heads

WHAT TO DO
1. Tie the string tightly to both ends of the 3 foot green stick so that it bows slightly.
2. Glue the two 'arrow heads' together over the tip of the 2 foot long stick.
3. Make a few ground rules for safety, then let the children try their bows and arrows...aiming for targets only!

SET A THANKSGIVING TABLE

MATERIALS YOU WILL NEED
    one placement and napkin
    one plate, fork, knife, spoon and glass
    white glue
    one 12x18" piece construction paper
    one 4x8" rectangle of scrap material
    one pre-cut cardboard knife, fork and spoon
    one paper plate
    one circle pre-cut 3" in diameter

WHAT TO DO
1. Discuss table manners, how to pass food, and proper table etiquette with the children.
2. With the materials you brought, show them how to set a proper table with real utensils.
3. Using the 12x18" piece of construction paper as the placemat, have the children 'set' their own table with the paper plate, and pre-cut knife, fork, spoon, and 3" circle, which represents a glass. Use the 4x8" material scrap to represent the napkin.
4. Once the children have practiced 'setting the table' a few times, have them glue each piece in its proper place on the construction paper placemat.
5. If you wish, add additional pieces to your place setting, such as salad fork, dessert spoon, or salad plate, so the children will learn where to place these also!

41

PILGRIM'S HAT

MATERIAL YOU WILL NEED
    two 12x18" sheets black construction paper
    stapler or glue
    scissors

WHAT TO DO
1. Cut one sheet of construction paper into a large circle to make the brim of the hat. Cut the center out to make a hole for a brim.

Brim:

2. Fold, then cut the second sheet of construction paper in half through the middle of the width to make two sheets of 9x12" paper.
3. Lay these sheets together to make a long 9x24" rectangle. Staple or glue the ends together.
4. Roll the paper into a cylinder which will fit the brim. *(see illustration)*
5. Make 2-inch cuts every 2-3 inches around one edge of the cylinder to make tabs to attach it to the brim. Staple or glue the top to the brim, finishing the Pilgrim's hat.

PILGRIM'S FEDORA

MATERIALS YOU WILL NEED
    one 9x12" sheet white construction paper
    stapler

WHAT TO DO
1. Hold the paper lengthwise and fold it in half.
2. Staple the edges on each side so that it is 4" high.
3. Fold the right corners at the top of the fedora over and staple them down.
4. Wear the Pilgrim's fedora to a Thanksgiving feast!

INDIAN VEST

MATERIALS YOU WILL NEED
    one large grocery bag
    scissors
    crayons
    glue

WHAT TO DO
1. Cut up the middle of the bag, then cut a round hole for the neck.
2. On each side, cut out an arm hole.
3. Draw designs on the Indian vest with crayons.
4. Wear it while you read the poem, "The Tom Tom," on page 17 of this book. Use an oatmeal can and a stick to beat the tom tom as you recite the poem.

PATCHWORK QUILT

MATERIALS YOU WILL NEED
    8x8" squares of muslin material
    various colors of fabric crayons or permanent
        marking pens
    needle and thread
    pins
    scissors
    strips of material to run along the border of quilt

WHAT TO DO
1. Have each child draw a design on his or her square(s) with the marking pens.
2. Stitch each square to the others in rows; then stitch the rows together to make the quilt.
3. Either sew a border or stitch the strip of material onto the edge to make a border of a different color.
4. Hang the patchwork quilt where all can enjoy the colorful artwork.

1.　　　　2.

3.

INDIAN DANCE MASK

MATERIALS YOU WILL NEED
 one 8x12" oval cut from a grocery bag
 tempera paints, a variety of colors
 brushes
 scissors

WHAT TO DO
1. Explain that some Indian tribes often would wear dance masks while they performed ritual dances.
2. Carefully cut out two eye holes.
3. Decorate the dance mask with bright designs and colors of tempera paint.
4. Hold the mask in front of face while performing the Indian dance found on page 27 of this book.

45

TURKEY HEAD PIECE

MATERIALS YOU WILL NEED
  one 1x18" strip of white construction paper
  stapler or glue
  one 1x6" strip of white construction paper
  one pre-cut circle, 3" in diameter
  one yellow triangle beak
  one red turkey wattle
  crayon

WHAT TO DO
1. Bend the 1x18" strip around the child's head to fit exactly. Staple the ends together so the child can wear the band.
2. In the front, staple the 1x6" strip onto the headband.
3. At the end of the 6" strip, glue the circle on for the turkey's head.
4. Glue on the turkey's beak and wattle. Draw the eyes with a crayon.
5. Put the headpiece on and recite the poem on page 14 and page 18 of this book: "Turkey's Move In The Strangest Way" and "One Fat Turkey."

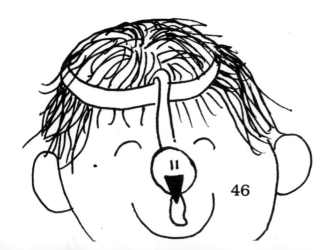

46

HAND PRINT TURKEY

MATERIALS YOU WILL NEED

> one 8x10" oval of white construction paper
> brown finger paint pre-mixed in a pie tin
> red felt tip pen

WHAT TO DO

1. Dip child's palm in the paint tin.
2. Press one brown hand print in the center of the oval with fingers and thumb spread wide apart.
3. Set aside to dry.
4. Draw eyes, beak, and wattle with the red felt tip pen.

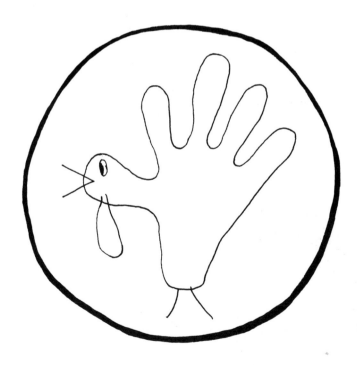

PILGRIM'S COLLAR

MATERIALS YOU WILL NEED
   9x18" white construction paper
   scissors
   scotch tape

WHAT TO DO
1. Cut the paper to the approximate shoulder width of the child.
2. Fold the paper in half.
3. Cut a half circle from the center of the paper for a neck.
4. Round off the outer edge of the collar to make a circle.
5. Cut a line up the middle on one side only so the child will be able to put on the collar.
6. Once the collar is on, tape the edges together so it will not fall off the shoulders.

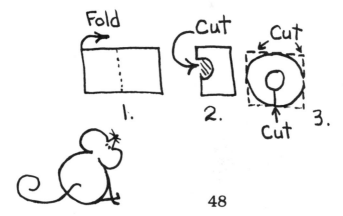

PAPER PLATE TURKEY

MATERIALS YOU WILL NEED

one white paper plate approximately 9" in diameter
one red wattle cut from 3-4" construction paper
one yellow triangle beak
two black eyes cut from construction paper
white glue
containers of red, green, yellow, brown and orange tempera paint
a brush for each color of paint
newspaper

WHAT TO DO

1. Lay down the newspaper to cover the table before painting. Paint 'feathers' all around the outside rim of the paper plate. Use different colors all the way around, if you wish.
2. Set aside to dry.
3. Glue the circle to the center of the plate for the turkey's head.
4. Glue the eyes, beak, and wattle onto the head.
5. Read the poem, "Turkeys On Parade," on page 18 of this book, or sing, "I'm A Little Turkey," on page 24 of this book.

49

INDIAN HEADDRESS

MATERIALS YOU WILL NEED
one 2x18" strip corrugated cardboard
one or more real feathers
stapler

WHAT TO DO
1. Measure the cardboard to fit the child's head. Make sure the corrugation is running vertically.
2. Push the quill of each feather into the head-band so that the feather stands up in the Indian headdress.

CLAY VILLAGE

MATERIALS YOU WILL NEED
modeling clay

WHAT TO DO
1. After you have talked about the way the Indians or the Pilgrims lived, the tools they used, and how they made their homes, ask the children to recreate either an Indian or a Pilgrim village using clay. Make sure they think about the smallest details, from making pots to stacking firewood.
2. Display your clay village as a reference. Add new details as you learn more about that time in our history.

Pilgrim
And
Indian
Games

INDIAN BLINDFOLD GAME

MATERIALS YOU WILL NEED
blindfold
one piece of fur material (or a sponge)
large lawn or blacktop area

HOW TO PLAY
1. Arrange the children in groups of 5-7 players.
2. Before you begin, explain this is a game the Indian children played very quietly..."and you should, too." It helped Indians learn to listen as they walked through the woods.
3. Blindfold one child and have him stand in the center of the group. Hand him the fur piece.
4. One at a time, each player from the group should sneak up QUIETLY and try to touch the player who is blindfolded before being hit by the fur piece.
5. If the person in the center hits a child with the fur piece,the child must sit down away from the game. The last child standing in the game should be blindfolded in the center for the next game. If that child has already had a turn, he or she should choose another player to stand in the center.

Variation: Have one person stand in the center blindfolded. When the person in the center yells, "Turkey!" all the players yell, "gobble, gobble!" The players must keep one foot in place at all times through the game while the person in the center tries to locate and tag them while still blindfolded. The last person tagged is "IT" for the next game.

PILGRIM MUSEUM

MATERIALS YOU WILL NEED
old tools, clothes, books, or anything from the old days which you would be willing to lend the museum.

HOW TO PLAY
1. Label each item. Explain its use. Make a list of the children who lent objects to the museum. Display them.
2. Pretend to take a trip to a museum. Appoint one child as the curator, another as the visitor to the museum. Or have each child explain his or her own display and how each item was used or worn.
3. If your community has a local historical museum, you might suggest the children visit it, or you can all go together.

RING ON A STICK

MATERIALS YOU WILL NEED
one pencil (Indians played with a stick)
one 8" string
one 1" pre-cut end of a cardboard tube
contact paper to cover the cardboard tube
(you will need one for each player)

WHAT TO DO
1. Tie one end of the string to the cardboard tube.
2. Tie the other end of the string to one end of the pencil.
3. Cover the tube with contact paper, making a ring.

HOW TO PLAY
1. Hold the pencil vertically in one hand.
2. Gently swing the ring up over the eraser of the pencil and try to catch it.
3. The object of the game is to catch the ring on the pencil.

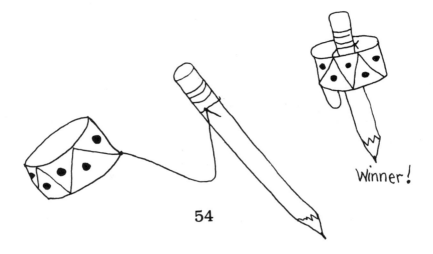

Winner!

TRACK
"THAT PESKY RACCOON"

MATERIALS YOU WILL NEED
a piece of soft, fake fur, or a raccoon skin
flat stones, three different sizes

WHAT TO DO
1. Lay out a trail for the children to follow by setting up stones to mark the way. Use the following patterns to give the children clues.
2. Before the children go out to track "that pesky raccoon," explain what the following stone patterns mean:

This is the trail.   Turn right.   Turn left.   Danger.

    Now, tell the children to go outside and follow the stone path until they find "that pesky raccoon" or or piece of fur.

3. The first child to find the "raccoon" is the winner!

Variation: Rub raw onion on trees. The children must find "that pesky raccoon" by following their noses down the path, smelling onion tree to tree until the "raccoon" is found.

55

THE BEAR HUNT

MATERIALS YOU WILL NEED
none

HOW TO PLAY
1. Start a rhythm which you will maintain during the entire game by clapping your hands, then slapping your knees.
   slap—clap—slap—clap—slap—clap—etc...
2. Chant the verse and begin the game. "I'm going on a bear hunt, a bear hunt, a bear hunt. I'm going on a bear hunt, a bear hunt today. Oh, oh! I didn't find a bear. I found a

   _____

   (Here each child takes a turn filling in what he or she found on the bear hunt. It can be ANYTHING!) on my bear hunt, today. But, that's okay. I'll try another day." *(Name next child who will have a turn.)*
3. Repeat the verse until all of the children have had a turn finding somethng on the BEAR HUNT.

Variation: For a class of older children, have them each remember and repeat what all of the other children have found on their bear hunts in order. The last player will have a lot to remember!

56

HIDE THE THIMBLE

MATERIALS YOU WILL NEED
  one thimble

HOW TO PLAY
  1. Show the children the thimble. Explain how it was used in the old days while women sewed and mended.
  2. Explain this favorite old game. One child hides the thimble in the room while the others close their eyes.
  3. When the thimble has been hidden, the other children look for it until someone has found it. That child is the winner. If necessary, give clues to the thimble's location by saying, "you are warm" when a child is close to it, and "you are cold" when a child is far from it.
  4. Whoever finds the thimble first is the winner and hides the thimble for the next game.

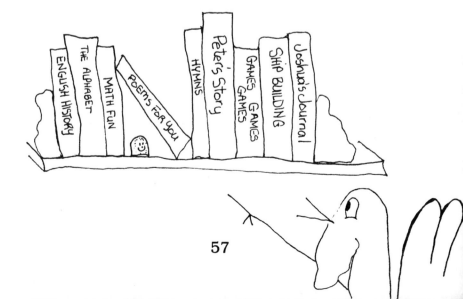

THE TURKEY TROT

MATERIALS YOU WILL NEED

turkey parts (head, body, legs, feathers made of flannel—the number of tail feathers will vary with the number of players on each team.

1 flannel board or piece of flannel cloth per team

a starting line

HOW TO PLAY

1. Give each player on the team one part of the flannel turkey. Each player should have a different part of the turkey.
2. Have all of the players on each team line up behind the starting line in a straight line. Each player should have a turkey part in hand.
3. Upon the signal, "GO!" the first player runs up and puts his or her turkey part on the flannel board, then runs back to touch the hand of the next member of the team. That player then runs to the flannel board and puts on his turkey part, then returns to the line to touch the hand of the next player. Continue until all the players have had a turn to run to the flannel board and the turkey is complete.
4. The first team to complete its turkey and have all players back in line is the winning team.

THE ACORN TOSS

MATERIALS YOU WILL NEED
>   ten acorns (you may use marshmallows)
>   a small basket 4-6" in diameter
>   one chair (or round of a log) to stand on
>   (Indians stood on round stumps)

HOW TO PLAY
1.   The children should line up one behind the other near the chair.
2.   The first child in the line should step up on the chair.
3.   Place the basket away from the foot of the chair.
4.   Hand the child ten acorns, one at a time, so he or she can toss the acorns into the basket at the foot of the chair.
5.   The child with the most acorns in the basket is the winner.

Variation: Give each child an acorn and a stick about 3 feet long. Have all the children line up behind the starting line. On the signal, 'GO!' all players must ROLL their acorns o the finish line approximately 10 feet away. The first across the finish line is the winner. Note: There will be no kicking, smacking, or handling the acorn. It must be rolled or guided with the stick.

WOUNDED KNEE RELAY

MATERIALS YOU WILL NEED
a starting line and a finishing line
...at least 25 feet apart

HOW TO PLAY
1. All players line up behind the starting line.
2. They must all lean over and grab their shin while bending their knee, and hold their leg for the entire race.
3. When given the signal, the race begins. The first child across the finish line with the wounded knee is the winner. If a player drops his leg, he is disqualified. (Don't be too hard on them,though! It is very difficult to run with a wounded knee!)

Recipes for the First Thanksgiving

61

COLONIAL PUMPKIN PIE

INGREDIENTS YOU WILL NEED

2 cups mashed, cooked pumpkin
   (or one 16 oz. can of pumpkin)
3/4 cup of sugar
2 t. ground cinnamon
3/4 t. ground nutmeg
1/4 t. ground cloves
3 slightly beaten eggs
1/2 cup whipping cream
1/2 cup milk
1 unbaked 9-inch pie shell
mixing bowl and spoon

WHAT TO DO

1. Combine pumpkin, sugar, spices, and salt.
2. Blend in eggs, cream and milk. Stir until well blended.
3. Pour into pastry shell.
4. Bake at 400° for 40-45 minutes, or until a knife inserted in center comes out clean. Filling may crack.

PIE CRUST

INGREDIENTS YOU WILL NEED

one 3 oz. pkg. cream cheese
1 stick margarine
1 cup flour
rolling pin

WHAT TO DO

1. Soften the ingredients. Mix together throrughly.
2. Roll out on floured surface. Place in pie tin. Makes 2 crusts.

PLYMOUTH APPLE DOUGHNUTS

INGREDIENTS YOU WILL NEED
4 cups buttermilk biscuit mix
1/2 cup sugar
1/2 t. cinnamon
1/8 t. allspice
1 cup applesauce
2 eggs beaten
shortening or oil for deep frying
electric skillet
doughnut cutter
sugar or powdered sugar for topping
mixing bowl and spoon
paper towels

WHAT TO DO

1. Combine applesauce and eggs. Stir until well blended.
2. Add biscuit mix, sugar, cinnamon and allspice. Mix until all dry ingredients are thoroughly moistened.
3. Knead dough 8-10 times on a lightly floured surface.
4. Roll out dough 1/2 inch thick.
5. Flour the doughnut cutter, then cut doughnuts.
6. Heat the shortening to about 375° for 2 minutes.
7. Drop doughnuts into the hot shortening, just a few at a time. Fry for 2 minutes, turning them once.
8. Remove them and drain the excess grease on a paper towel.
9. Roll them in sugar or powdered sugar. Makes about 15 doughnuts and doughnut holes for young Pilgrims to enjoy.

PILGRIM'S CORN MUFFINS

INGREDIENTS YOU WILL NEED
1/2 cup corn meal
2/3 cup flour
3 T. sugar
2 t. baking powder
1/2 t. salt
2/3 cup milk
1 egg
1 t. melted butter
mixing bowl and spoon

WHAT TO DO
1. Mix dry ingredients
2. Add milk and egg yolk and beat for 2 minutes.
3. Add butter. Mix well.
4. Bake in a moderate oven for 25 minutes.

CORN ON THE COB

INGREDIENTS YOU WILL NEED
     fresh ears of corn
     water
     salt
     2 T. sugar
     butter
     knife
     large kettle and lid

WHAT TO DO

1. Remove the husks and silk from the corn.
2. Place the corn in the kettle. Fill the kettle with just enough water to cover the corn.
3. Add a pinch of salt to the water.
4. Add the sugar to the water.
5. Bring the water to boil. Turn down the burner and allow the corn to simmer for 10-20 minutes or until tender.
6. Drain water off corn and serve. Be sure to butter salt the ears for a delicious treat!

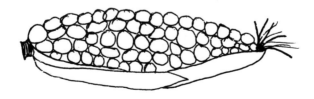

INDIAN PUDDING

INDGREDIENTS YOU WILL NEED

    4 cups whole milk
    2/3 cup yellow corn meal
    2 beaten eggs
    1/2 t. ground nutmeg
    1/2 t. ground cinnamon
    1/2 t. ground ginger
    1/2 t. salt
    1 cup maple syrup
    2 T. butter
    3/4 cup raisins
    saucepan
    mixing bowl and spoon
    2 or 3 quart baking dish, well-greased

WHAT TO DO

1. Scald the milk.
2. Mix 2 cups of milk with corn meal. Stir until a thick paste is formed.
3. Add the remainder of the milk and stir.
4. Cook the milk and corn meal in the saucepan over a low heat, stirring constantly for about 10 minutes or until the mixture is smooth and thick.
5. Beat the eggs and add them to the mixture in the sauce pan.
6. Now stir in the nutmeg, cinnamon, ginger, salt, butter, maple syrup, and raisins.
7. Pour the mixture into the well-greased baking dish.
8. Bake uncovered in medium or slow oven until set, or about 1-1/2 to 2-1/2 hours.

NAVAJO FRY BREAD

INGREDIENTS YOU WILL NEED

    2 cups white flour
    1 t. salt
    2-1/2 t. baking powder
    2 t. dry milk
    2 t. shortening
    3/4 cup warm water
    bowl
    spoon
    towel
    knife
    waxed paper
    rolling pin
    frying pan (electric)
    shortening
    salt or honey

WHAT TO DO

1. Mix the dry ingredients in the bowl, then mix in the shortening with your fingertips.
2. Add the water and work into a soft dough.
3. Cover and let rise for 15 minutes.
4. Roll the dough into a long log. Cut off small pieces of dough about the size of golf ball.
5. Roll each ball between two pieces of waxed paper to flatten.
6. Fry in smoking-hot shortening in the frying pan.
7. Serve with salt or honey once the bread has cooled for a few minutes.

TEA FROM THE WILD

INGREDIENTS YOU WILL NEED

Go into the woods and gather one of the following to make the tea: Douglas fir needles, Redwood needles, pine needles, Yerba Buena leaves, or sassafras roots. (no stems please)

sauce pan

water

cup

strainer or sieve

sugar or lemon if you must...but no milk

WHAT TO DO

1. Place 3/4 to 1 inch of leaves or needles on bottom of sauce pan.
2. Fill the pan with water.
3. Bring to boil.
4. Let it steep for 5-10 minutes, or longer for stronger tea.
5. Pour the tea through a strainer as you fill each cup.

COOKED CRANBERRIES

INGREDIENTS YOU WILL NEED
    1 pkg. cranberries
    1/2 cup water
    2 cups sugar
    large saucepan
    stirring spoon
    bowl

WHAT TO DO
1. Place cranberries and water in sauce pan.
2. Bring to slow boil and cook. Listen to the berries pop!
3. Add the sugar and stir.
4. When the berries are thick and most of them have popped, take off heat and serve.

APPLESAUCE

INGREDIENTS YOU WILL NEED
>2 large apples
>3 T. water
>sauce pan with cover
>knife
>food mill, sieve, or blender
>spoon
>bowl

WHAT TO DO

1. Core and slice the apples.
2. Place in the sauce pan with the water. Cover.
3. Simmer 10-15 minutes, or until apples are tender.
4. Press the apples through a food mill, sieve or blender.
5. Cool...then eat! Makes about 1 cup.

Your
   Own
      Turkey
        Notes

Credits

Educational Co-op

Silverfork Elementary School

Redding Co-op Preschool

Louise Taylor

Mike Huber

Heidi Huber

Charlie and Gillian Trumbull

Trudy Stevens

Linda Witczak

Linda Jones

Ron Schultz

---

*Thank you
for all your input and ideas!*

The Turkey's End ...

... Unless, you have Ham this year!